The Gray Door

THE GRAY DOOR

PATRICK JAMIESON

Ekstasis Editions

Library and Archives Canada Cataloguing in Publication

Jamieson, Patrick
        Gray door / Patrick Jamieson.

Poems.
ISBN 1-894800-54-0

        I. Title.

PS8569.A4697G74 2004   C811'.54   C2004-904409-5

Acknowledgements:
Cover Art by Ken Horn
Typesetting: Louise Beinhauer, Wordworks
Author photo: Jamie Jenkins

Published in 2004 by:
Ekstasis Editions Canada Ltd.   Ekstasis Editions
Box 8474, Main Postal Outlet   Box 571
Victoria, B.C. V8W 3S1   Banff, Alberta ToL oCo

The Gray Door has been published with the assistance of grants from the Canada Council for the Arts and the British Columbia Arts Board administered by the Cultural Services Branch of British Columbia.

Dedicated to those muses of the future
Martha, Hannah, Sarah Jamieson &
Sarah Butler (and their mothers)
plus Norah Lorway

Contents

PART THREE
SOME LONGER POEMS

WEDDING QUARTET

Gray Door

Where I lived in Sydney, Nova Scotia, in a small apartment by myself, during most of the period when these poems were done, I looked out, from my kitchen table, upon a gray garage door at the rear of Sydney Millworks Ltd. The purposes of the building must have changed because the door now faced onto a grassy fenced-in area; and I never saw it open.

Let No Word Fall

(for Hannah)

Religion is no substitute,
Other side her soul.

Ten days pass without;
Young creative sensibility sown.

Birth six years past,
Every photo shows her

Hearing sounds, painting call.
Let no word fall.

Stellarton Station

Time casts atmosphere waiting,
Time between, time until.

Train has left Truro gaining,
Time ticks, baggage waits, still.

Benches wait hearing noises;
Blend distant voices resignation:

To still cars snow observation;
To Sydney, slowly, destination.

Fallen Angel

"In alchemy, angels are a symbol of sublimation." – J.E. Cirlot

Fallen angel, where are you?
You haven't fallen that far.
Speaking together of redemption
Sunset in your car:

A dictionary of angels,
You'd never thought of such things.
Fallen angel, I know you;
Sky's panorama white with wings.

James Dobson

At your funeral weeping
Waiting by your wife
Saying simply its so hard
I feel like an onlooker
Observing instead of feeling
But that's my time & situation.

At Tracadie the angels perch
On gateposts of the cemetery
While they have small wings
They're prominent to view.

And Wind Snaps Pane

You arrive, asking which is the door;
Then enter, looking askance,
Oblique questioning askew.

I search out colored ashtrays,
Surmising you're on your way West.

The comment passes
You are increasingly lucky
Not to have a husband;
And I can see that.

You seem the least interested
In knowing where the dead angels
Are that they used to hide.

I cannot tell what you can see
Of me: Sitting in the chair
As you do.

As she spoke of her eyes,
I felt unspeakably near,
As if she were kin.

She then said
Goodbye, Goodnight
Three times or four:

You stand obliquely remote
By your black car, by its door.

Port of Call

Do you remember, Sylvia,
How you stopped the take-off
Of that jet, because of the
Anxiety of your narrow
Premonition?

I didn't love you any more
After that because you hadn't
Treated me with kindness.

Its true, your father died
The next day, and we should have
Stayed on so you could go through
With the funeral but
I expected the possibility of
Forgiveness.

My sister and my mother
Went over to the funeral
Together tape recording
The sound of the service.

In My Stead

They were forced to draw lots
For my replacement
And it fell to you, Matthias.
I didn't hang myself. I escaped
Merely into the passing night.
Who could take my place with her?
Her, with no husband,
And two delightful urchins, bare.

Once I entered her door
— she hadn't answered —
And, she was in the tub
With them, naked, I imagine
Though I did not see.
They are having some time
With their Mother,
She called down the stairs.
I went away for over
A quarter of an hour.

Later, they set me in the company
Of the princes of my people.
You see, Matthias,
You cannot know
How well things can turn out.
And you, what have you done
That is so significant?

Anarchist in Love

"With the sea at your feet,
and the phoney false alarm." – Bob Dylan

You who taught me to love rain and gray,
Feel their beauty, and the depth of my soul,
Call them beautiful, feel meaning of that word.
You who taught me to speak the truth,
Fearlessly honest, being with you.
You who met me on every plane,
Traveling across continents, to breathe,
To sigh out final poison of disappearing wound.
Provided the map to your yard, key to your pane,
Professed love undyingly, meeting ardor
Time for time, intensity as it came.
You've taught me to dream again,
In blue face and yellow jacket: To follow
An inclination to trust the natural course
Of the law, by being an anarchist in love.

Ersatz Asperity Partners

"With the flesh like silk and your face like glass…"
Sad-eyed Lady of the Lowlands – Bob Dylan

We were out of there by 12:12,
Scooting around in the new Golf,
You driving, running your noon-hour errands.
Deliberately putting my hands on you
When walking your dog, asking you
To marry me again, approaching the door in.
Doing an inventory on Wedgewood
Blue houses, your usual noon-time
Pleasantness with me, and everyone
Else on the street. Looking at houses
We could own on our combined aggregate
Salary like real urban professionals.
I said we'd need one as large as the
Light yellow rambling place on the
Esplanade for our combined aggregate children.
You said six between us was enough,
We don't need to produce another just for
Fun. Putting the dog in the car,
Roaming back to your place of
Work where I posed the profound
Question in dark glasses, either
As a poet or as a real person
With pure passion. It was then
You consented to kiss me on the
Cheek and later I wondered if you
Would do anything out of character,
Like purchase that negligee to hang
Out in together, and hang up in my
Closet after. It all must be happening
Because we are probably saying goodbye
Again.

Just Disguised

I've watched some water
Wash by wider bridges
I've dallied with sandwich
Where calm waters rear to run

Lain beneath July leaves
Learning August ripeness
Sky has moved blue
Midst angel mucus

Her nudging register
Nuance summations
Sufficient sweetness
Allusions to affection
Her endearing nibble

We're still like that —
Simply disguised

Beauty of the leaves
Lifts her focus
In its being
Breeze stirs leaves
She commands to be
Naturally.

Duke Dining

Soon she'll be flying, not so flustered south
To New Orleans, but now she's simply here with me.
First feeding bread to ducks, talking to an 'old thing'
Dog, walking to lunch at The Vista, place she knew about
But had never been, heard all about from a friend.

Her usual Caesar salad shared, her chowder
My soup of the day; skipping that pie today.
Me more relaxed with her than ever before,
And that's relaxed. Since she's slightly stretched
Today, must be some shift in me. Tell her of adventures
Captured in some poems, symbols she'll accept.

Ask her about the wedding, other changes, plans
All settled she says: "Smiling he returned to bed."
Relaxed we are covering bases, good goodbyes are said.

Rear Window, Front Access

(for Bill Johnson)

Its six o'clock in the morning
A milk truck goes by
One car turns a corner
Another climbs a hill.
A cab takes the same corner
Red lights blinking on.
One month into winter
Finally Sydney is still.

I'm looking out the window
The moon is two thirds there
Houses in the back yard
Huge and dark and silent
A Japanese car goes by.
They all go by on George Street
Glenwood is ignored.

The lights are on in Wentworth Park
But don't reveal anyone there
The bridge is lit the ice is orange
That milk truck comes back by.

I wonder where the policemen are
If its been a quiet night.
Someone finally travels Glenwood
Going the other way
makes the short s-turn
Disappears by the park.

Turning my eyes inside
I see your painting there
They bring me a certain comfort
Speak to an inner me.
A truck comes along, makes the turn
Goes right by the house
Me I'm searching for some symbols
To help me get in touch.

Where Did You Go?

(for Elizabeth May)

I hoped I was being honest with you
With those messages on the page
It could have been too much for you
Chances always were that I'd quit.

Its just that I saw this path in a dream
Where we were treading along in a rage
Something kept saying to let you know
For my part we could probably fit.

You still go to the tower each day
I hear of your growth on the stage
Its clear you'll survive, you're doing just fine
From the perspective here where I sit.

If you ever do wonder where I went to
Its on the bottom of the very last page
Of that final letter after your decision
With no message I knew that you'd quit.

Lucille in New York

Even hypnosis requires will power
         he said. We were caught in traffic.
My mind was saying:
         No Leo sun
         No satin sheets
         No low-court victories
         No labour struggles.
This is the middle of the road.

The shadow of the unicorn
         made me wonder about her
         again. Why we never kissed twice
         yet she put her lips on cigarettes daily
         hourly regularly with lipstick red.

Her postcard was art deco
         of the Chrysler Building
         the unfinished nightclub
         the unfurnished restaurant
         the unfocussed movie.

She called in the morning
         resolutely refusing his inquiries
         leaving a feeling throughout his day.

In the gallery he had nine minutes
         to get through, deciding to return
         after the festival.
         He still had regular images
         of her smiling enigmatically
         talking matter of factly
         avoiding her face.

In his recall, he asks her a few direct questions
        and only a few are about New York City

Out of traffic now
recalls desire
not a lot of lust.

Nothing For You

Others felt flooded, by gifts, sentiments;
Realities they didn't desire to receive.
You, you design societies beneath your hat;
Expecting nothing, its delivered; accepting that.

You wave, passing by, noting forlorn face.
Not in vain, calling up, bestowing grace.
I sail on, utter goodbye; on occasion singular.
You don't mind, expecting shortly, separation only.

I've gone before, to get away; presently, its over.
Things shall subside, I surmise; usually there are others.

Soon we'll part, in retreat, having promised nothing:
Me I offer — having missed — absolutely nothing.

In March

At six o'clock the sun shines going down
On a brick wall adjacent, days are lengthening
In March, though darkness soon ascends
Revealing stars like points of light in the sky.

This is March when sap runs like middle age
When time itself shortens as the second half
Of one's life suddens and approximates abbreviation.

At six O'clock day is still prolonging itself
In the form of light from above falling on brick
Walls like ivy or shadows of leaves in autumn.

This is March before the gardens grow, women dream
Of the colour of flowers while men scan catalogues.

This is March when gray cloaks give way to yellow
Windbreakers: And wind blows wild and west.

From An Afternoon Divan

A lot of excitement in the sky today
Hawks, crows, gulls moving in patterns
I can barely discern. Surely this isn't
Going on all the time, it's the light
The day, the time of year; or my eye.

   Gulls drifting in this window's upper pane
   In the blue and yellowing sun. Houses fill
   The lowest inches — Gray poles, yellow trees
   Sunshine makes blocks of light. In only
   Moments afternoon will begin to go off.

      Swallows squeak, beckoning farewell day.
      Gray bands of cloud covers the top of a telephone pole.
      One much taller tree still green reacting to wind's
      Shakeness; Gables all seem aimed the same way.

         Hawks circle swiftly through the central panes
         Golden dove of peace bobbling in the breeze.
         Every time I come home carrying a new mood
         Darkening of the day. One totally leafless tree
         Spreads outstretched in praise like an eccentric man.

Part Two

You Are My Wings

When we danced, we were as one person,
One creature, one the body, one the wings;
Androgynous together, reaching in together
To be attached, form one being, like an angel.

I reached within your openness like a jacket
To touch your back below where wings
Would be attached. In moving together
We seemed to fly; glide, your term
Word which says floating away, above limits
We knew before encounter, which held us.

Each before shedding some confines, self-imposed,
Which wouldn't allow previous introduction
To the unity we felt waltzing with our hands
Shifting in each other's, thighs parallel:
Your gray jacket like my wings; My strong back yours.

Gemini Twin

You, in responding to my minor display
Of vulnerability, some naked wholeness
Of a soul, with an invitation, through
Your own past art, with some naked lines.

All your numbers seem to add up to
Four: This according to intuition
Is simply fine. Our poverty is paired.
Your bedroom where emerges your hidden
Self who resembles at first little
Me, from my reading now well disposed.

Your bedroom decorated in rented
Period pieces, furniture you've left
Behind. Your daughter a Libra
Though your only one. What you
Display of your self, photos on the kitchen
Table where the completeness of Four
Was Charted moments before, revealing
It is true, a very well preserved Thirty Six.

I like your lines, I like your triangle,
Your darkest circles, your perfection
Of sorts. There is evidence in this
To me we were destined to be friends:
Glimpses too of dancing selves
Perhaps more than desired, or expected.

Model

Roamin' 'round your large kitchen, as I do
Out on Wicklow Road, there is this photograph of you;
In a kaftan modeling I call it
That made me wish to see as much more.

And speaking as we do
In that endless introductory way
As you say, never actually arriving
At any firm place, either beyond
Or more.

Ranging through our variously
Shaped rooms. Perhaps it was
Something in response to a poem
But you decided to show me more
And roaming as I do, following soon
You went into your back bedroom
Withdrawing I saw from the lowest drawer
A full portfolio of photographs
Modeling of you.

It was your art at the time:
I was enthralled with how
Much more of you there was to see
Kaftan trailer and all matching
My own nakedness of poetry free.

Anticipating Getting Better

(Unicorn Union From a Dodge)

"It was time to be himself again, to see
If the place, in spite of its witheredness, was still
Within the difference." – Wallace Stevens
(Extracts from Addresses to the Academy of Fine Ideas)

Once in a while,
Tooling around the streets of Sydney,
One glimpses windows alight at dusk
Resembling Klee paintings — square blocks of colour —
And yours, Miro.

I saw her walk the opposite way, yawning at noon;
In yellow rain boots
On Charlotte Street, with our common friend.

Months I avoided her doorway, laying low;
Months of being away. All those short days,
Purity of fragrance of butterscotch.

Someone walking by your house in Halifax,
The past five minutes — noisy as horse trotting,
Heard from second-story sitting room,
Sitting.

Sounds to be in the room; through the window,
Horn above middle of equine face. Untamed
Yet: Terrifying, loyal and alone.

2.

The restaurant, it turned out,
According to one chap's reliable
Daughter, was not what it appeared
To be in the various implicit commendations
Of close friends.

Direness in the very cheesecake he nibbled;
In its butterscotch topping.

Seated in your living room, Miro. Tapies,
In your place; your favourite easy chair,
Crossword puzzle still on the arm.

Sneaking a peek at an endless fun postcard,
Addressed, undelivered, to someone's relatives.
See your admission that something will not occur
In this your lifetime — not for fifty years.

Downstairs, beneath here, your landlady
Dwells in intimacy with her second husband
(Who drinking doesn't trust your brush.)
In her kitchen she has calendar portraits
Of twelve fabulous creatures; Strange horses.

3.

What are you doing for the next fifty years?
You asked her, attempting to mend her car.
"Oh, not much," she replied in earnest.

At Gooseberry Cove

At Gooseberry where a gray angel
Appeared overhead at dusk time,
Sunset saw a pink tail, spreading wings.
I saw my destiny on earth in blue,
Adjacent to the navy roiling sea.

And yet, when emerging from the sleep,
Emerging from the immaculately smelling
Cave on wheels, looking up to gray angel,
I saw another side of destiny, in the west,
Higher up, blue like a sky, on the day

A girl child was born, travail over.
Relaxed, refreshed, renewed, driving off
From this place where it all intersects.
Earthy blue, sky gray, angel pink tail.
A white tail disappears into the bush.

Listen Again

(for Joella Foulds)

As I stated in the studio, I had to turn away
From the beauty of what you sang then,
Above Charlotte Street; preferring ugliness,
But discovering since — recovering since —
A taste for the local; a taste for your
Capacity to speak in photographs.

The sun behind you a black sky.
The sky above you a black curtain.

All those women who are your friends:
What you said about the pain and the gain.

There are trees in your past;
Carnations on your shadow;
Red chairs in your room.

You're not asking questions in the morning now.

In the deep winter, I climbed closer
To the words from your blackboard
Blue face, beneath your bright and
Earnest; your black and blue garment.

Your sophisticated unsophistication.

Summer will arrive eclipsing even
Spring; salient you'll sing.
I can hear you now — open again —
Clear as water from a crystal glass
On stage: Listening again.

Your friend in her red tam, pregnant.
Speaking of your father and the plough:
Put another season's promise in the ground.

Written on a Velvet Venus

"When we should be enjoying bliss that beckons,
Tears appear before my eyes, in yours.
We are halted as with a wall, which I resent
But nothing of you, who is innocence discovered."

In May, we were simply introduced as fallen angels,
Searching for words, names, signs, titles: dictionary bound.
Heading for a ferry; poems and paintings followed.
Cloud banks on the boat spoke to me,
Someone ancient named Herb in Hiding to you.

For you, I believed it could come through painting
Herb. In July, there were calls;
Following letters: great letters, great cards
Anticipating a final resting place for Fidelity's Finest:
Our code continued. August brought a decision

And you were introduced to Duke, the fourth woman
And feminine father. You were like a pilgrim laughing
Your way to ecstasy, whether you realized it or not.

By September, you were in your gray space studying law;
Looking at papers for three years, you said, midst muffin
Breaks, Madonna movies. It was better that way.

To Catch the Light

(for Sarah, Hannah, Martha)

The clouds — the incredible clouds — of New Brunswick
Have become eclipsed by these Prairie ones.

The constant and precipitous butterflies
Of August.

The children choose two of three:
Merry-Go-Round, Ferris Wheel, Choo-Choo Train.

The one in the purple bathing suit stands in the corner,
The one in the blue, waves. The one in the green
Has disappeared from sight.

Daughters, "godders," sisters,
Riding backwards into the dark of the tunnel.
The children scream with excitement.

Re-entering the light, rainbows surround
The spray of the sprinklers.

Three sit on brown bench:
Purple, blue, green.

The clouds on the building
Are in square boxes.

In the donut shop, sitting beside the three-year-old
In summer dress with hearts.

Out of the Hudson's Bay bag,
Her new sweater fell on the sidewalk,
Running to the corner to catch the light.

The entire pattern of high drifting clouds
Moved as a whole.

I Don't Think It Will Be That

(For the Water Walkers)

I don't know whether it was
The poolside mirror nailed
To a brown fence, or
How she said in her three-year-old
Innocence: "I don't think it will be that."

Or merely the conjunction of the two
And the sense, once again,
Of a red umbrella being raised
Like a symbol of a covenant
To tent the episode of the day
When three young, young girls
Walked on water.

Or perhaps it was the passage
Of yellow music through an early
Mode of evening while mother
Dozed on a green couch, and
He leafed raptly through an ancient grammar text.

That was classic and anachronistic
When he used it twenty years before:
Its abiding memory, the friend who sat
Behind him throughout high school,
Who died in prison, falsely accused.
And the table manners of poetry
It promised. In blue.

Never Say No

(Janet, of course)

Holly wrote, saying your friend and your mate
Are verging on marriage, beyond the shadow of
Your fading. I recover how you used to say, after
Your own waitress days: a refill's always welcome.

Some like Holly (and maybe me) wondered about
That stuff, if you didn't imbibe it too much.
Her own health as robust, she misses me, she
Wrote: Her ache for you is designed in her dress.

It was a picnic table, in a hospital quad, where
Holly came through, the hall, across glass walls,
Out into the open air, promising to be mutual,
Performing as premised; hotel angel hair.

Holly wrote, she and Brad are married from November,
For a second third time, revolving it in or out.
When you were alive, walking up hill: Bistro bound,
Explaining his special role, Harold were his name.

Where you held minor court, mere bohemian than garrulous,
Then I recall, recovering from mine own alley Garden
Days. I received after after Holly's fame, her name tripling
Off your lips, refilling good, no-ing sunshine of your tongue.

Blessing As He Passes

(To Janet Robertson)

She was a friend of mine:
A gypsy soul in a ship adrift.
Only God seemed to know her code.

Furious with her physician,
Stimulated by rapping on the door;
Her body let her down, though, in the end,
Like every friend.

Many wished to spend it that way, but
She got angry at it spillin' away.

When I asked for appreciation,
She couldn't admit to understand;
As I'd done this complete reversal
From what she'd been led to expect.

Now her lover's mother is her lawyer
And I no longer feel on trial.

While her lover finishes his beer,
I search in my coffee dregs.
It's ashes to ashes, dust to dust —
Caring for her a hungry crust.

You're just part of it now, he said,
Something she'll not get beyond.

Many simply spend it, I thought,
She, she's slipping away.

46

On a bed in a railway hotel,
I'd stroked the angelic hair
Of her college friend, recalling
Reconciliation while the mirror
Portrayed a chair.

She dwelled in her space; and time:
Islands of escape, coast of clearance —
You will recall, Beyond your final call,
Fall and curtained hall,
How I read at her funeral,
Cared about her
And grew through it all.

Slaying the Dragon

Our clothes are patterns we
Put on to defuse the issue:

Uniforms we adorn to avoid
Change. We wear them not

To change, to sidestep growth.
Look in your wardrobe to see

What you refuse to become.
Before, we used to imagine

We took our clothes off to sin;
Now it is clear, the truth is

Just the opposite. In the sky
The curious cirrus clouds are

A dragon on his back, with his
Feet straight up in the air.

In the chapel, the sun against the
Stained glass, gives an appearance of

Dragon claws, descending: Five talons
Each, on a Chinese Emperor's ornaments.

How we do train our minds to be
Steel boxes aimed at each other:

Bestowing our blessing on this one.
Condemning that one, beyond our control:

Deciding who is holy, intelligent,
Simple, all things fine, worthy of

Our esteem; in comparison, in our
Constriction hardly glimpsing the

Good we leave undone, unimagined.
And, in our attire, we adorn ourselves

In avoiding the issue of our self.

Our Owl Nights

"In the Egyptian system of hieroglyphics, the owl symbolizes death, night, cold, passivity. It also pertains to the realm of the dead sun, that is, of the sun which has set below the horizon, and which is crossing the lake or the sea of darkness." – J.E. Cirlot

You write on hokey owl paper, in your words, while
To me it is a reminder of our upstairs / downstairs
Cold nights, of willing death to the false start
We knew; embraced, let go, in your small rented
Urban house, through the windows of which I experienced
Some of your sun; alone, in day time, on the floor,
Meditating on your spirit — cold and passive, of necessity;
Like a twelve-year-old child, though actually a childless
Mourning forty, who sleeps with her huge golden dog, Watson;
Now dwelling with her in rural cottage: New man in your life,
John Smith; house-bound, what you need for nocturnal delight.
Our nights alone together, me on your couch, you in your bed
Upstairs, were best spent that way; any other spending
Would have been premature, for both our body, and our mind.

Yellow Bath

Josie, do you recall, as I do, 1965
When your cousin Albert studied
Medicine in this Atlantic city?

We stayed one time in this hotel.
The friendly doorman: Was his name
Horatio? We occupied this very room
Or one just like it, with its muted tone.

You said that the angles,
The grays — even the noises in the hall —
Held this muffled quality.

A yellow bathtub in such a
Context seems happily appropriate.

A period piece of a hotel room,
With twin beds and yellow curtains.

Where did you say Albert lives now?
His daughters, the babies: Did you say
The red-haired one is on the stage?

And the yellow-haired younger one
Is in the military, like her Father?

Their uniforms are sharp and gray.

Brass Angel

Listening to radio, Peter's Signs. Early Saturday
Evening; you sipping tea in a Peter Rabbit mug.
On the mantel, clock hesitated permanently
6:37 p.m. I'm holding a thin mug of tea.

You are somewhat approaching
An appearance describable as wan
The immediate after tone of drink.
Massah, the puppy, wears three collars
Drags his hind end across the carpet
Toward you, where his eyes…

                    After the radio show
Which we both agree is very fine; tea finished
I have two questions: one about nuclear arms;
The other about Albert Schweitzer's photograph.
Then the interview might be over. Lunch
Is arranged as a possibility after you tell me
That photo, while nearly famous, is Uncle Norman's
Work, among various enterprises, including peace.

On the mantel also is a brass angel, which
I do not ask you anything about though you do say
The picture of Margaree Harbour mist is your work
And something of home for here. Finally there are
Two moulded storks balancing off the space
Under the arrested clock. On the radio, someone,
The husband, said, "Calm down, Elizabeth,
Nobody is going to get shot," I look up
At the brass angel.

Part Three
Some Longer Poems

Closer to the Peacock

Some Longer Poems

Peacock: On the Roman coins, the peacock designates the apotheosis of the princess, just as the eagle does of victors.

The peacock's tail, in particular, appears … as a symbol for the blending together of all colours and for the idea of totality. This explains why in Christian art, it appears as a symbol of immortality and of the incorruptible soul.

The common motif of two peacocks symmetrically disposed on either side of the Cosmis Tree denotes the psychic duality of man … drawing its life-force from the principle of unity.

In the mystic horology, the peacock corresponds to dusk. In Hindu mythology the patterns on its wings, resembling innumerable eyes, are taken to represent the starry firmament.

J.E. Cirlot, from *A Dictionary of Symbols*

The Opposite

In the morning, you drive up before eight
Saying on the way, I am being quite quiet.
After the service, we sneak off
For a coffee before you head for the ferry,
I say to you, from James Wright's poem,
Besides you are much more intelligent than me.

From then we agree to say the opposite of what we mean,
I am habitually telling you how good you look.
We arrange how I will receive Anatole France's
The Revolt of the Angels, while I recall, inadvertently,
My father saying furniture will be no problem.

The women who wait in service are beautifully revealing,
But even they could not eclipse you,
In my view no-one could.
I do not suspect how writing this poem
Can reveal to me how happy I am.

I ask you for a parting kiss,
Wander off to get Dad his coffee, without looking back.
Upon return, there is this empty space where your car was.
I look over an $18.31 receipt from Il Buco,
Where we had minestrone after your final exam.

Presently I am anticipating a quiet week
While you are wrestling with your interior angel.

Perhaps I'll visit that art gallery
Where you said you just could not buy
A green, stuffed fish for my brother,
Taking a Klee poster instead.

Years ago — if I'd met you years ago —

I would have suggested the Klee,
And I can imagine you saying
The green fish was just the thing.

2.

At Mass, you liked the radio coming over the PA system,
I commented on the Monsignor's style,
While three teenage girls sat at the opposite end
Of the pew from their parents, directly in front of us.

The middle one, in colourful jeans, slid over
To kiss her father at the eucharistic peace.

You kept letting go of my cold hand,
Saying at coffee, how the priest would
Give up on me if he saw me with my arms
Around such a drug addict.

I say how could anyone say that,
After glimpsing your face.
Arriverderci, you smile, on the church steps,
After kissing my father good-bye.

You say I appear angelic
And that my little horns are showing.
I say you are still ugly and stupid,
And will doubtless become more so,
In my view.

No Interest or Disinterest

She pours the drinks, four colours at a time.
Gold specks on her black jumpsuit, move in line;
Red leather belt, thongs dangle, touch her thighs.

Talks over the bar, with cop off his beat.
Minor gold Medusa, leans head back easily,
In chat, and chatter; He consults a sheet.

Sydney Chinese food palace hostess,
Says she's feeling hyper with change;
Getting no sleep. And that's why
She's cleaning the glass shelving,
High above the bar, she explains.

Oriental statues, symbols behind the glass.
She says she's been riding motorcycles,
Swimming in the ocean: Travelling in her
Bikini, she states. Speaking easily with
Waitresses, mentioning something, laughs.

Slender Medusa, broad smile, sipping coffee.
Customer, trying to write a poem, muses:
Given the chance, I'd treat her well:
He dreams. She openly wonders, her eyes
Say. Tells her friend she's on her way
To Halifax Monday; he's just been.

They talk engagedly, when he pays the bill:
Surprisingly to him, holds up his end; she
Hers. Continually, open-ended, goes on.
Ends when someone else inevitably comes along.

He wonders, wandering home.
She escorts someone to their table,
Returns to clean the glass.

Magic Canso

In Halifax, someone named Patrick,
Who killed someone named Patricia,
Is going up on trial.
That truck, just ahead,
We're running on the same fuel:
And Halifax, we're running that way.
I don't know my parents anymore;
Or my brother, or kids, too;
Now that I'm in love with you.
Those flowers by the road,
In the near-fall, light-purple
With yellow-centres, I noticed.
They're kind-of gray.

There's a ship in the canal,
Called *Magic*; there's a canal,
Around the ship, called *Canso*.

Just beyond Stellarton, at Green Hill,
Is the Magic Valley, where driveways
Resemble crushed gravel;
And necks crack in relief.

Coming into the city, what did he see:
A young guy walking like Jackson Browne;
An old guy teeing off.
He's feeling some old realities,
A vitality entering his skull.

2.

Arriving at the Mother House,
Lamp posts had been painted yellow.
Pleasant enough to follow. All day
He used yellow trays; sat in yellow chairs.
Entering a secret chapel balcony, he thought:

You feel the angels in this place;
Golden ones guarding the dead Christ;
Michael in stained glass with red wings,
Piercing the tongue of the serpent Satan.

You can peer down on the tabernacle
From above the covenant even.
Marble floors and candles make you
Conscious of some invisible forces.
Outside, jet engines roar, in the sky,
Audible in here, going past, for now.
Me, I lounge in a pew, with an orange
In my hands; gazing on an angel who
Is holding back the father's knifed hand.

Twelve Hours Past Midnight

Guardian angel felt a trifle bad
About the quality of His evening with you,
Saturday last, at Joe and Nicole's.

There was good talk, and wine and candles:
You drained His glass once,
Speaking in the descending dusk with Joseph;
While He hovered in the light
Of the kitchen, with Nicole.

Domination of Black, and His peacock story
Explained: Who is at my window? He asks.
The ideas of penetration, possibility
And distance — also symbolic of consciousness,
Or getting on with things (as you might say)
In spite of some feelings,
And Domination of Black.

It's something for the bathroom,
She suggested, searching 'neath the sink,
For a bar of white soap, in a basket;

A similar act of contemplation.

Though it was her neck and throat
That spoke most deeply to Him
That lingering mid-May evening, about
That long table, in certain dress.

He hadn't said, "Let me sit facing the Sun,
You could sit over here beside Jocelyne."
It wasn't appropriate, but

God, it's amazing, your economy.
One of the last lines in a recent note read:
"I continue to celebrate how easy
You are to get along with, and I
Hope to talk to you real soon."

They are having a few minutes with their mother,
She hollered. "What I have come to realize
Is God has no favourites."

Two Restaurants

I

Seated facing the window at noon,
He saw her walk by La Gargotte;
Looking at the restaurant
As if considering entering.

Or perhaps wondering if she should go in,
But not understanding why.
Dismissing the thought as funny
And passing by. He considered
Going after her but didn't.

II

Certitude stops short of entanglement.
He stays beyond his friend at Kamal's,
Refusing the lift home. Taking a chance
On hopping a bus later, accepting her
Conversation; transparently interested
In her offer of dessert.

When he asked for more hot water,
Carrying the pot to her, placing
It in her hand; he felt to be approaching
Her passageway, successfully at last,
Glancing behind him,
In the hallway. She'd sent him on
Ahead, in the dark, she put her hand
On him, getting out of the cab.

He'd looked at her across the perfection
She contained, telling her: The café
Wall's painting he'd looked over searchingly
Was titled *Certitude*. She held the key,
He was in the dark. The light
Was behind her, coming up the stairs,
She approached him as if there was no difference.

He'd never been there before when
She sent him back downstairs for something
He went on becoming accessible
Discoverable; unentangled certitude.

Wondering about him a few days
Afterwards, she didn't expect to see
Him come in again, pervading
Her presence as promised. He couldn't
But thought of her himself
For a longer while when in similar
Circumstances; as dusk descended.

      III

She felt drawn to enter each shop,
Dawdling too much, wondering why.
She meditated on changing restaurants.
Feeling strangely uncertain for a moment.

Apotheosis of a Princess

(Red Peacock Remembrance)

You never knew
What would come
Out of him. Always
On the sideline standing.
He didn't care
To respond.
Red turtleneck
On a summer mower.

His neck; her red
Hair different
Eyes not blue-green.
Midnight dancing
Approximately New Year's
Eve exactly what he felt
For her. What she said,
Projected her beautiful
Whimsey figure fulness,
Figuring. Waltz slowly,
It is supposed to last;
Meant to last forever;
It will have to last for ever.

At midnight,
He recognized what she meant to him.
Long remembering still
Feeling who she was
For him.
He never knew
What could come out
Of himself.

She was no blonde.
After you hear this
Your collection can be complete,
Your recollection is over.

He would often recall himself
In a red-turtleneck before
His neck went. He did
Her family's dishes
While waiting for her
To appear. Ducks appear
Out the window, over the sink —
She herself appears
In an unbelievable state
Of dress; her face,
He won't be able to forget;
He won't wish to forget;
He knows the word epiphany;
He loses the term transformation,
In his mind, he hears the sound
Apotheosis.

(she told him, while watching television,
or she told him when not watching out,
she had spoken with her dead grandmother)

An angel had visited her saying everything
Was all right, coming out of her closet,
When she was merely a little girl.

He and she spent time in the graveyard
Adjacent her parents' rural home. He got
Locked in the freezer of her father's
Store. She was not too impressed.

He hadn't cut her hair, certainly not
Her red hair. He refused to cut his own.
No poetry. He constantly wore a red leather jacket.

He read in the dictionary of symbols:
Peacock is the symbol of apotheosis of the princess.

Primary Colours

(Catching Up On My Dreams, in four parts)

Nancy, on the beach. The Beaches, winding crescent sand.
Waves catch her gaze. Sadness, realism, face beautiful.
Pregnant, she says, assumes its his. OK, ties that bind.

Off to her parents' home in city. Dad is seated on crescent
Bench in garden. Mother tangled in garden vines.

Meal coming up. Dad waiting reflectively
Not pleased with younger man; won his
Daughter's favours.

He warned her about the fate of her aunt.

Makes him nervous. Derided nervous cough.
Supper served near freeway. Hot dogs.
Splatters ketchup on white trousers.

She's not remote; present.
Father says he doesn't see himself on the cutting edge
Because Toronto is like many North American
Cities…

II

I saw you go by, in pink hat, burgundy winter coat,
Not looking up at the train; thinking to yourself.

I feel about you what she feels about me.
The clear desire to save and contemplate; adore.

I'm speaking metaphysically, obviously.
We go to the donut place where she and I
Ambiguously began; a faint hope persists.

In an empty frozen field, a shopping cart
Lies on its side. When I leave this region
It will be on a yellow train, like this.

The police brought him to the train station,
Continually telling him to behave himself,
An unnecessary warning from what was perceived.
In a woman's white coat, he stood in line.
On the train, he painted his nails red;
The familiar fragrance wafted into the aisle.

Seeing you walk to work, looking,
Albeit inaccurately, disheartened;
I want to say to her it is over
Between us.

Not anything that can be done
This morning but sit, but rest
And gaze out the window to the white
And the forest; watch for animal tracks.

Where did I see you there
In unconscious commentary
On my inner life...
The neglect of poetry.

Is it corrupting? Is it distractedness?
She knows it has to end. There's no hope
With either of you for different reasons.
I told her what the one who isn't a nun
Said about being in love with part of me.

On the way to see the bishop
And a priest. What was I doing
A year ago, or two; where will
I be in another year?

The fella in the white coat walks by
Saying something about an Express.
On an incline, a 4x4 is parked beside
The classic, middle-distance, middle-class home.
Who was it said something about
Wanting something better for herself?

Near the north central mall
Is an exact replica of the donut shop
Where it all ironically began with us,
And her, but not your yearning
For you, like in a dream.

Today is the middle one, Helen's
Birthday… in the summer, faced
With a decision, she said, over lunch,
Part of me wants to go, but part doesn't.
Toward dessert, she announced she would go,
Comparing her dilemma with the others':
Their moral dilemma of choice — realizing
Not so much the responsibility of choosing
Right over wrong, as living with the consequences
the baby, Margaret, liked me enough to jump on.

Eventually, it will come to an end,
She doesn't like me to say that.

"Do you remember when we took that
Bus ride together, along a longer river
Route, to Saint Robert," I'd written before.

Through the ancient window, the blue bank
Calendar reads January 18. Eighteen is a
Special number today, Mercedes said over
The radio waves — Brave New. Her aunt and
Uncle live here, and Doris from across the hall.

Montreal change in Truro, Halifax.

What is going to happen with us?

Basketball hoop deserted, stringless in snow
Covered field. Barn, white, has red sliding
Doors.

All this sunshine, the sun is the sky.
It pours through these moving windows.
We take it for granted, not worshipping
Thoroughly. Nature takes its course.
Gravity is working, to pull us down,
Hold us in place. The sun makes one squint,
Missing much of what is passing
On both sides — blue white brown green.

Not how but when to say to her
I wish to pursue other relationships.
I shall not be so nasty then
Late at night when manner is unbearable
To my corrupted sensibility.

The rusted bridge, the ancient ferry,
The clutter of ice, the natural pattern
Painted in the surface of the stirring
Water. Cables hold the platforms on. I
See the stone beneath the ice;
I see the dock beneath the snow.

I have to clear a space, I have
To endure your stare from afar,
Your gaze across the table, from the
Chair at the end of the bed where
You sit to prepare yourself,
To get yourself ready, to stay.

I've wanted to bring myself as a gift
To someone who turned out to be you.
That is what there is to say.

All those long Sunday drives
When I should have been on the train
All those long drives
When I was sick and getting sicker.

I wanted to bring myself as a gift
In order to be healed by your care.

III

Nan, Nan in a pastoral setting,
Far removed from the city, from
Even Peterborough. Nan pregnant,
Returning to the context of her
Father. Her mother in more remote setting,
In the matrix of her upbringing.
Her real beauty emerging, her
Authentic self allowed — how she
Signalled that, turning pride —
Fully to luxury, narrowness, self.

No, I've never gotten go signals
There since … the one unheard of
Except remotely, who appeared working
Nailing up plastic sheets near her home,
Her nest, her yard, where I was invited in.

In the station yard, stationary.
Another bare track appears, the snow glistens.

IV

He was invited to sit with two men,
Men who were laughing out loud.

As I left their car, car with the snack bar.

Another man, in this car, snores loudly
Just behind the seat that I have chosen.
Across the aisle, a chap in black eats an apple.
Me, I'm going to gaze out the window.

My coffee looks like her tea did at breakfast,
Unstirred, pale, hot, round, liquid.

A stream, there, looks like a road
Curving under a tiny bridge. It must
Be a stream, not a river. That is theology.

Today, where the sun has come, the sun
Has decided to pervade. I chose the right side
To see that, feel that, know that, become aware
Too. This isn't the Ottawa airport balcony,
This isn't a donut shop. This is a moving train.
The voice of the common people drifts back.
The voices. Voices like my own, though
Not written down, not even by me.

The man in the woman's white coat
Is fortunate to be who he is and
Accept it. Something others don't have.
It was not he who left the political book.

V

I Like To Be Alone

You and your father are one.
You and your father shall continue
To dwell happily together in the same
City. He took you to clubs, to hear jazz,

To galleries to see art, to his office,
To work. He delivered you to school,
All your parts. You, for your part,
Fiercely defend his right to live
And work and be; in a red Volkswagen.

I was lonely but I was not your father.
You and your father are one. He will
Accept your babies more than others,
Than he knows.

VI

I cannot really make out her face
In the station; too far from the frieze.
A yellow line crosses her mouth,
She moves away with a large white
Tam on her head. Oh I doubt she is
Going to the movies.

The ice heaved back away, cracking
Itself in the effort. The snow and
The ice is not pretty; it is beautiful.

VII

This is taking shape, as in 1976
This long poem of tracing and sight.
This short train with a third ear
For the Shriners' party. As the train
Moves along in the sun, there is
A parallel caterpillar of white squares
Reflectively moving alongside on the
Snowbanks and gulleys and trees.

Wedding Quartet

No Calls at Noon

WAITING

In this restaurant, overcast day,
I can barely see the figures on the street;
Just the forms of women walking away:
Their hair, determines their sex;
Their image, determines my response.

Curtains, layers of cloth, and lace,
Obscure the view, trigger recognitions
On an obscure level, for sure:
And more deeply familiar, somehow.

Haunting consciousness, like a shadow
From Childhood: In sand caves,
Using stolen smudge pots, for illicit
Light, stolen from around enormous road holes;
There so people wouldn't fall in.
We were so young, smoking,
Lighting illicit fires, endangering lives;
Though not our own, feeling
Cosy and secure, for sure.

A bus moves away, outside the window,
Two young women hurry by.

LATER

After you leave, there is this settled feeling
Where there seems to be more light outside.
Inside, and it could have been the hug, I wonder
Who is on the horizon, will lead me to venture.

You arrived with your kwick copies
Of wedding invitations; handing me mine,
After folding it the way it will fit
In the special envelope. You depart saying:
Be cool, act cool, it will go just fine.

I sit, looking through the curtains, and veils,
Feeling it is all changing for you;
In the way you would have it go.
You have departed mentioning a worrisome letter
From your mother, left unopened over a week,
Imparting with me a disturbing image
Of some visiting, historical priest,
Who, using your attic room, picked his nose,
And wiped it on the wall,
So your mother had to blame it on you.

Wedding Photographs

(To Bernie and Kari)

Kari met me inside the door
Of a huge yellow house
Where I never had been
(Georgie'd let me in)
With news of the silver rose
Synchronicity written
On her wedding face.

A spell was cast
In Betty's magical
Apartment. All through
Her meal we were
High as the proverbial
Kite from the feeling
Given.

It felt like some biblical
Wedding celebration.
Every symbol seeming
To point to important
Realities beyond
The moment: Our cup
Running overful.

Table was set for four:
Betty serving, hovering
Like a guardian angel.
The specialness she felt
Lighting from her lips,
Showing in her eyes; so
When I read those lines
From 1928, written by Teilhard de Chardin,
(as if for you two)
Rolling mist was in yours.

Georgie showed some tears herself
In yellow dress, blue belt.
Bernie handsome in lemon vest
And tie. Kari beautiful dressed
In black and white suit, gray
Scarf at her throat, gray stockings
Too.

My mind seemed carried away
By symbolism, as usual, noting
Butter in the shape of a shell,
Sign of a prosperous journey;
Roses signifying completion,
Consummate achievement, perfection.
George saying she hadn't
Realized it was such fun.

Betty's camera not working as well,
We waited beyond the feast;
Salmon-lobster soufflé,
Crescent croissants, tantalizing stuff;
For Ken to come, to cut the cake;
When he'd take real photos
Of you for posterity, and parents.

We made it to the courthouse
On time, where the judge was waiting.
He'd composed a pretty good talk,
Everyone thought; nothing, Kari said,
She couldn't live with. O'Connell,
His name, gave us a couple of copies
Of the text. Earlier he's missed
The point entirely when Kari'd told him
She was keeping her own name,
Just after the signing,
Midst tears streaming down her face.

I'd leaned over to see you place
White gold rings on the fourth
Fingers of your right hands.

You'd first met this judge
When he brought his old black dog
To have him put to sleep;
Patting him cheerily on the head,
You'd said, before returning
To adorn his black robes;
An image in a Colville print.

At the yellow house, upon return,
Georgie's pup, Teddy, looked to have
Stepped out of such a painting too;
With blue scarf tied about his neck
In celebration.

I'd shut the doors after we'd entered
The wedding chambers, room 229;
Georgie and me signing with you,
Giving our North End addresses,
Charlotte and Glenwood Streets.
Wet umbrellas lay open at the back
Of the room where your covenant
Was declared, for all to know, and
For us to seek some shelter within,
In some specific way ahead, and offer
Some; umbrellas like some bright
Coloured tents your lives represent,
To celebrate April 16th post-Easter
Yellow and blues.

Waiting, after, for copies of O'Connell's
Talk, I spotted a bunch of unopened
Daffodil buds lying on the counter,
And noticed back at the yellow house
A framed photo of opened daffodils
Mounted on the far wall adjacent
To the wide, slightly-opened windows,
Which leaned outward into a heavy rain.

Back at Betty's more coffee and cake
With Warren who'd arrived
With those two red roses, winning joviality,
Constant embraces, on an obvious high;
On a happy courthouse visit for a change.

There were stories like Bernie's mannequin
One; about shopping at Simpson's
For his suit where the soon-to-be-wed
Clerk was helpful in the extreme.
The one who pointed out the judge,
Who happened to be strolling through.
Betty's story about the sixty-dollar
Moxham Castle desk. The mysterious
Lady at the Court House who commented
On your comeliness as a couple; and
The continuing ensuing jokes about
All the weight Duke soon would gain.

Betty's self-composure, and that
Wonderful laugh, passed on to her daughter.
Tales of their brilliant, live-wire
Husband and father, whose passing
Silently speaks to them in the eyes
Of numerous owls, all about the place.

Kari's own tale of the 'wonderful kaleidoscope'
From her birth-of-the-gazelle New Orleans trip.
We drank up the remains of the Grayman champagne,
And Kari tossed the blue garter just for fun,
And I ended up with it in my pocket.

Something changed in me that day,
Some sense of a new possibility of hope,
Symbolized by roses of perfection;
Their optimistic yellow in this wedding photo
Of your combined slender eloquence,
Of Kari's gentle healing weeping,
Of your mutual surrender, and
Bernie's trembling aplomb, which
Just as surely gave his emotion away.

But it's yellow roses somehow I recall,
Though in actuality none were there.
Your earlier coincidence of roses
Brought them to mind, but those,
Like your rings, were silver too.

A gold band encircles you-two now,
I mean you-one now, circle signifying
Some arrived-at level of natural completion:
A yellow wholeness, in my mind,
Approaching, and promising, gold.

At Ingonish With Carol Anne

(To Kari Dukeshire)

I thought I could drive up
As far as Neil's Harbour,
But the fog wouldn't allow
Anyone to see anything;
And the enormous road equipment
Had the highway blocked eerily
In the fog, a short young woman
Held up a red sign sayin' STOP.

So I drove back to the beach
Where one can listen to waves lapping,
Hear the constant clicks
Of the quartz clock in the car;
Feeling oneself relax:
And remember.

I thought I was coming way up here
To get in touch once again
With where we'd been
And remember her. But it's you,
Our faithful guide and companion,
I keep seeing — in the road sign,
Warren Lake, and in the form
Of a woman dressed as you do,
About your size and length,
Moving among rocks and stumps,
When I turned in the thick fog.

I'll go back down to Ingonish Beach,
Near the cabins, closed now, where
We stayed, in #17, near the tourist home
Of blueberry pancakes, where the woman
Mistakenly called me her husband.

Now, you have a husband, as I'd always
Thought you did, but in name now too.
I was one of six at the wedding,
Four plus you two — and the jovial judge.
And shall recall it long, though casually
Entering into it, as witness; our church
Person, you half-joked one day at lunch.

I entered casually, what did your friend say,
Comfortable to be with; rising for the occasion,
Yet only because it proved to be the epiphany
Anticipated, what you deserve; as guardian companion.

Not arbitrary action, this trip, rather
A call received, to speak to some folks
Regarding the health of their souls, I suppose.

This time I stayed over, at the Glebe House,
Instead of simply visiting the pastor,
Alone, in the morning. Yet today too
I awoke feeling full of joy and innocence,
As I knew I would; as I did that day.
Still the shift holds some significance.

This trip too, I have that symbol dictionary,
At which you invisibly raised your eyebrows
Then; yet have learned to like, if not respect.

Perhaps respect: after all, it was you
Who rushed to the door, the wedding morn,
To point out how your earrings perfectly
Matched the brooch given by the mother of
Your friend, my matching comfortable witness;
And wasn't that a perfect happy coincidence?

So, shortly after this, I'll return to the West Coast,
And you two to the mid-west, if we can call it that.
Not knowing what the future holds, perhaps
I shall be able to spend promised time with Carol Anne;
Perhaps we shall converge again on these shores
Nine years from now, as also promised:
To witness what time has wrought from this Atlantic
Episode.

Horse Hurt

(Dashed Dreams, Failed Hopes)

The call came into the clinic about 10 pm,
And we drove over by midnight;
Duke saying on the way
How stallions always made her nervous;
And how she hoped he wasn't a jerk.
I thought she must mean the owner, at first;
But he turned out to be a nice guy, in her phrase,
The horse that is, she repeated it to him time and time again;
Holding his wounded flank.

A chestnut-coloured quarter-horse,
New on the farm this day,
Had jumped into barbed wire
Tearing six or seven wounds
Mostly in his front legs,
With a little one on his face.

The rancher turned out to be a nice guy too,
Full of ideas and questions of Duke,
While she slickly got down to work, in khaki coveralls.
He was getting his money's worth.
Sometime after one, after most of the wounds
Were bound, when I was starting to fade,
He asked me what I did, and the topic turned to that.

He said he had always wanted to write a book;
And as Duke said on the way home,
He'd obviously done a lot of thinking about it.

There was a book he was bound to write,
Even had a title picked out,
Dashed Dreams and Failed Hopes,
Or something like that,
About a farmer he'd known.

2.

Driving through Northern Ontario,
On the way to Lundar, Manitoba,
I kept seeing three horses in a group
And the thought I had was
That when I got to Lundar —
The symbolic centre of my journey —
I might well see a cluster of four
Upon arrival at their animal clinic:
A white former army barracks
Attached to a yellow clinic building;
And sure enough, through their living-room window,
The prairie summer sun revealed seven of them in a field
Across Highway #6;
Three plus four, I said to myself.

3.

In the afternoon, Bernie and I
Had driven about as far as we could go
Within the clinic's service area,
To look at a dairy cow with a paralyzed tail.
The earthy farm women, one barely beyond a girl,
Contrasting favourably in their openness
With rural Nova Scotian women where I'd been;
Where Duke and Bernie, and I had met.

4.

British Columbia, at my journey's end,
Occasionally, observing horses,
A dapple white on black leaning through a wire fence.

Remembering another stallion, rearing by a roaring fire,
Along the Fraser River, last Christmas when
We had breakfast with her wealthy, comfortable parents,
One Sunday morning in the rain, in a restaurant
As different as Knight and Day.

They simply smiled at what I had to eat.
Now I feel like someone in a line-up; and
The difference I feel, is more than night and day,
About how she seeks their approval
Using boyfriends, or whatever, as symbols
Of rebellion and decay.